THE TRAIL OF TEARS

An American Tragedy

by Tracy Barrett

Perfection Learning®

About the Author

Tracy Barrett is a direct descendant of Elizur Butler, a missionary who was imprisoned for trying to help the Cherokee. She lives in Nashville, Tennessee, with her husband and two children. She teaches at Vanderbilt University. *The Trail of Tears: An American Tragedy* is her ninth book for children.

Cover image: *The Trail of Tears*, painting by Robert Lindneux, **Woolaroc Museum, Bartlesville, Oklahoma**

Image Credits: ©CORBIS p. 33 (top), ©Peter Turnley/CORBIS p. 60 (bottom); **Cherokee Indian Village photo reposited, Museum of the Cherokee Indian, Cherokee N.C.** pp. 14, 38; **Museum of the Cherokee Indian, Cherokee N.C.** pp. 32, 34, 40 (top), 43, 54, 63; **Courtesy of the Oklahoma Historical Society** p. 40 (bottom) (negative #125), p. 58 (Mrs. Redbird Smith Collection, negative #681), p. 59 (top) (Mrs. Redbird Smith Collection, negative #688), p. 59 (bottom) (photo by Grant Foreman, Thomas-Foreman Home Collection, negative #20588.13.16.1), p. 60 (top) (Mrs. Redbird Smith Collection, negative #687), p. 61 (photo by C. R. Cowen, C. R. Cowen Collection, negative #19687.IN.FC1.16.20), p. 62 (photo by C. R. Cowen, C. R. Cowen Collection, negative #19687.IN.FC1.16.13), p. 65 (top) (photo by Grant Foreman, Thomas-Foreman Home Collection, negative #20588.14.6); **The Philbrook Museum of Art, Tulsa, Oklahoma** pp. 15, 37; **The Walters Art Gallery, Baltimore** p. 20–21; **From the Collection of Gilcrease Museum, Tulsa** p. 50–51 (*Trail of Tears*, 1957, black and white wash by Brummett Echohawk, accession #0227.1487); **Western History Collections, University of Oklahoma** p. 57

ArtToday (some images copyright www.arttoday.com); **Library of Congress** (some images copyright www.loc.gov); **Corel Professional Photos** p. 18 (bottom); Michael A. Aspengren, illustration p. 10

Table of Contents

Timeline

c. 11,000 B.C.	Humans arrive on North American continent from Asia.
c. 1000 A.D.	Mississippians dominate future southeastern United States.
1540	Hernando De Soto is the first European to arrive in the Cherokee territory.
1684	First treaty is signed between Europeans and Cherokee.
1730	Chief Attacullaculla visits King George II.
1738	Smallpox devastates the Cherokee Nation.
1782	First large-scale move of Cherokee to the west.
1802	Compact of 1802 legalizes forced removal of the Cherokee.
1808	Dragging Canoe's party moves west.
1813	Cherokee join Andrew Jackson in defeating the Creek.
1819	Cherokee law forbids sale of Cherokee lands to non-Indians.
1827	First Cherokee constitution is passed.

1828	Gold is discovered on Cherokee land.
1829	Georgia declares Cherokee laws invalid.
1830	Indian Removal Bill is passed.
1832	United States Supreme Court declares Cherokee Nation a "domestic dependent nation."
1835	Treaty for Removal signed by small number of Cherokee.
1836	Treaty Party leaves for the West.
1838	The Cherokee are rounded up, and the Removal begins.
1839	The Trail of Tears ends.
1846	Peace is declared among various Cherokee factions.
1984	The Eastern and Western bands of Cherokee meet formally for the first time since the Removal.

Introduction

To Die in One's Country

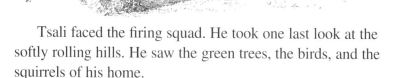

Tsali faced the firing squad. He took one last look at the softly rolling hills. He saw the green trees, the birds, and the squirrels of his home.

The men aimed their guns. They were Cherokee like him. Most of them wept. He knew they were about to take his life. But he knew they had to follow the soldiers' orders, just as he had to resist them.

Right before the bullets cut through his body, Tsali spoke. He said to his killers, himself, and future generations, "It is sweet to die in one's country."

Tsali was a peaceful man. He lived in eastern Tennessee with his wife and large family. They hunted, fished, and grew crops just as their **ancestors** had done.

They were content to live the way they had been brought up. They were friendly with the white people. But they kept mostly to themselves.

The family thought they would live out their days in the hills of Tennessee. They hoped that in death, their bones would lie with their ancestors' bones in the **ancient** burial grounds.

Then the soldiers came. They ordered Tsali to leave his home. He refused to listen to them. After all, the white people had already taken most of the Cherokee land. What could they want with more?

The soldiers had been threatening to force the Indians out for years. But they hadn't really done it.

Many Cherokee had married white people. They lived like white people. They attended Christian churches. Their children went to school with white children. They blended in with the white community. How could their neighbors, friends, and even relatives turn on them? This made no sense.

But now, the soldiers meant business. They charged on to Cherokee land. They snatched up the Cherokee and forced them to leave their homes.

Tsali and his family were scared. They didn't want to go to a strange, dangerous country. So they ran away and hid in the forest.

But the soldiers found them. They captured the runaways and led them off to a **stockade**.

On the way there, one of the guards was rough with Tsali's wife. Tsali lost his temper. The usually gentle man, his sons, and some friends fought with the soldiers. One soldier was killed.

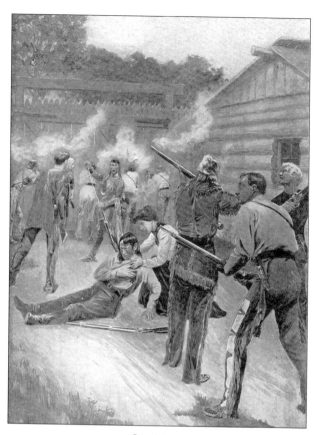

Stockade

The Cherokee men knew they would be **executed** for the white soldier's death. So they ran back into the hills. They hid again. The women and children were locked up.

General Winfield Scott was in charge of rounding up the Cherokee. He heard about the death of his soldier.

Scott told everyone that if Tsali and his sons would give themselves up, he would let the rest of the runaways stay free. And they could remain on their land.

Just as Scott had hoped, the men in hiding heard about his offer. Tsali had seen the number of soldiers. And he knew the size and power of their guns.

Tsali knew his people were no match for the United States Army. He also knew that sooner or later, he would be found. Then he would be executed for the death of the soldier. At least he could save the lives of his sons, brother, and friends. Tsali and his fellow runaways went to the stockade and **surrendered**.

General Scott ordered Tsali, two of his three sons, and his brother to be put to death. But the general was true to his word. He allowed the rest of the Cherokee to stay in their homes.

They were luckier than most of the Cherokee. Others were forced to take a long, dangerous trip. It was to a

General Winfield Scott

strange new land, hundreds of miles away.

No one knows much about the story of Tsali. Many say the story is truly a myth.

Some of the believers say he was not married. So he had no wife to be treated roughly by a soldier.

Others claim a friend of Tsali's had actually killed the soldier. Tsali took the blame for him.

Still others say he did not surrender to Scott's troops. But he was tracked down by other Cherokee hired by the soldiers. Then he was executed without speaking any heroic words.

Whatever the story, Tsali has become a hero to the Cherokee. He is also a hero to many people who believe in standing up for their beliefs. He has become a symbol of freedom.

Who were the Cherokee? And who forced them off their land? The answer lies in a tragic story. It has become known as "The Trail of Tears."

The Principal People

The story really began about 11,000 to 13,000 years ago. It was near the end of the **Ice Age**. For thousands of years, the earth had been in winter.

But now, the Ice Age was coming to an end. Mountains of ice, called *glaciers*, were melting. Huge mastodons and other mammals were moving down from the north. They were followed by human hunters.

The tribes made their way into America. They were what we now call the *Paleo-Indians*. They were among the earliest people on this continent.

The Paleo-Indians settled in what is now the southeastern United States. For thousands of years, they lived in the forests, plains, and marshes.

Later, other groups of American Indians moved in. Some were accepted by those already there. But some were not.

The groups often fought. Sometimes the new groups won. Then they killed or drove out the earlier groups. Sometimes they lost. Then they were killed, **enslaved**, or chased away.

The last group of Indians to move into the area were the early Mississippians. They arrived about 1,000 years ago. The main Mississippian divisions were the Creek, Shawnee, Yuchi, and Cherokee.

Anthropologists have given the name "Mississippian" to these Indians. They feel this really wasn't a group. This was more of a trade network. Anthropologists don't know what name these Indians used for themselves.

The largest division was the Cherokee. They called themselves *Ani-Yun'wiya*. This means "The Principal People." No one knows for sure what the word *Cherokee* means. Some think it comes from a word in the Choctaw language, *Chillaki*. And they think it means "cave dweller."

Others say it comes from a Muskogee word meaning "people of a different speech." It could also be the Cherokee word *Tsalagi*. It is short for *A-tsila-gi-ga-i*. It means "Children of the Sun."

The Cherokee settled in what is now Georgia, Tennessee, and North Carolina. But where they originally came from is a mystery to historians.

They probably lived around the Great Lakes at some point. Their language is similar to the language of some Indians there.

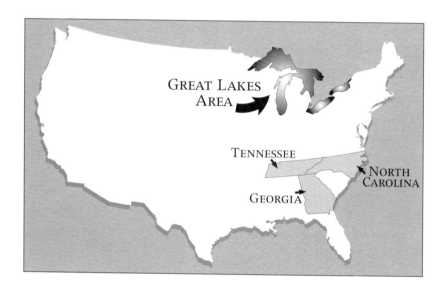

Cherokee Life

Some estimate there were about 25,000 Cherokee. They lived and hunted over 44,000 square miles of territory. Their hunting grounds extended from Georgia to Tennessee.

The Cherokee protected their right to hunt and farm in that area. But they did not believe that they or anyone else owned this land.

All the cultures who were involved in the Mississippian network were corn growers. They farmed as well as hunted.

Sometimes the Cherokee fought over who had the right to an area. But there were often hard times. So people from different tribes hunted and farmed side by side in peace. This way each group had enough food to survive.

The Cherokee lived in about 60 towns. These villages were usually built near streams. The streams supplied water and fish. Farmers could also **irrigate** fields during dry times.

Some larger Cherokee towns had 50 houses. The towns also had gardens and a grain storehouse. A high wall defended the village from attackers.

The houses were built around a central square. Most buildings were made of wood. Each family had a hothouse. This is where they would steam themselves for cleanliness and for religious reasons.

Cherokee families were not large. This was partly because many infants died. Everyone belonged to an extended family, or *clan*. Clans were made up of cousins, uncles, aunts, nieces, and nephews. The seven clans were called Bird, Wolf, Deer, Wild Potato, Long Hair, Blue, and Paint.

The most important building in each village was the seven-sided council house. Meetings were held there. Some council houses could seat 500 people. People stayed with their own clans. One clan sat on each side of the huge building.

Near the council house was an open space called *the square* in English. The square was used for religious celebrations, parties, dances, and games.

All decisions concerning the town were reached by agreement, not by voting. Discussions sometimes lasted for months. Everyone had to agree.

All the adults in the town were equal. The leader was just like everyone else. He had no more say than the others.

An English visitor thought this equality was wrong. It was so different from his own English ways. He said, "The very lowest of them thinks himself as great and as high as any of the rest."

Each town had its own government. It dealt with local matters.

There was also a central government that handled problems for all the Cherokee.

Every year, local leaders met at Chota, a town on the Little Tennessee River. They discussed war, trade, and other important matters. They came up with rules that all the towns had to obey.

LITTLE TENNESSEE RIVER

CHOTA

The Cherokee had great respect for the elderly. Also, they thought everyone should take care of the poor or sick.

The work of both men and women was necessary for survival. The men hunted, and the women farmed. Often the women worked all day. Their babies were strapped to their backs. The women grew corn, beans, potatoes, squash, fruits, herbs, and flowers.

Some of the plants were used for eating. Others were for making medicine. Flowers were grown for their beauty as well as their usefulness.

Women prepared animal skins. Then they made these skins into clothing. They also built the houses. The houses belonged to the women.

Women were the heads of the household. They decided everything that had to do with their families.

Men made the weapons and hunted. They also ran the government.

Cherokee at War

During war, the *Kalanu* led the Cherokee. This war chief had a council to advise him.

The *Beloved Woman* or *Honored Woman* also helped the war chief. She was chosen by the people.

The Beloved Woman's most important job was to decide for or against war. She also decided whether captured enemies should be killed, set free, or made into slaves.

Captives were often held for a long time before being killed. They were sometimes treated roughly. The Beloved Woman could free them. Or she could make the other Cherokee treat them more kindly.

Some freed prisoners were let go to make their way home. Others were traded for Cherokee who had been captured by others. A few were adopted.

The Cherokee often battled other American Indians. But they never fought among themselves.

Some wars were fought over who controlled the hunting grounds. Others started when a Cherokee was killed by a member of another tribe. The death might have happened by accident or in a fight.

Cherokee religion said any death had to be **avenged** to keep life balanced. Sometimes these **vengeance** battles grew until they involved entire villages.

Boys were trained from an early age to be warriors. Part of their education was to watch the torture and death of captives. The whole village, including the children, participated in the executions. The agony of the victims was a valuable lesson to the boys. They learned it was better to die in battle than to be captured.

The Cherokee were feared by other American Indians. Once during a war, a group of Yuchi soldiers were trapped on the banks of the Hiwassee River. They all committed suicide. They feared being captured by the Cherokee.

By the early 1700s, the Cherokee had forced the Yuchi, the Creek, and other Indians out of most of their hunting territories.

Cherokee Religion

The Cherokee believed there always had to be a balance between life and death. They celebrated that balance in the Green Corn Festival.

This was a time for starting the year over. For this festival, houses were cleaned from top to bottom. This symbolized a new beginning. The people forgave anybody who had done something wrong to them in the past year. Elders or medicine men led the celebration. Everyone feasted on roasted corn.

The Green Corn Festival was only one of several special ceremonies the priests led. The elders were also healers. They kept busy looking after their people. Therefore, they did not have time to hunt or fish. They were supported by other members of the town.

Some Cherokee Festivals
• First New Moon of spring
• Green Corn Festival
• New Green Corn Festival
• appearance of the October New Moon (Nuwtiegwa)
• establishment of friendship and brotherhood
• "Bouncing Bush" Festival

Religious ceremonies were a normal part of daily life. The line between religion and daily life was very thin.

A ball game similar to lacrosse was very popular. It was played for fun and as a religious game.

People played flutes, drums, and rattles for enjoyment. But they also used the instruments to make sacred music.

Dances were an important part of Cherokee religion. Some were also performed for recreation.

The Cherokee believed in the Creator, *Yowa*. He had created them out of the ground. So the land on which they lived had a special meaning. The land was where they came from. And it was what they were made of.

The land was also where their ancestors were buried. And it was where they, too, would be buried one day.

The Cherokee didn't believe in "owning" land. For them, the land and everything on it belonged to *Asga-Ua-Galun-lati*, the Great Spirit.

The Cherokee believed all creatures, including humans, were related to one another. Many still hold this belief today.

Wilma Mankiller was a great chief of the Cherokee. She once said, "We are one small part of a very large family that includes the plant world, the animal world, and our other living relations."

This circle of life included not just humans, animals, and plants. It also included the *Nunnehi*. The Cherokee believed the Nunnehi were beings like people. But they were tiny. They were thought to be only two feet tall.

The Nunnehi were rarely seen. They were seen only by children. These tiny beings lived in hidden places. Caves and hollow logs and spaces behind waterfalls were favorite dwellings. People would leave them food. In exchange, the Nunnehi would help children with their problems. They would lead lost people home.

The Nunnehi also took the dead to the underworld. The Cherokee believed the land of the dead was to the west.

So the Cherokee feared the West. This is where the earth and sky came together. It was called the "Twilight Place."

The sun set there every day. It seemed to die. Then it was miraculously reborn every morning. The West was where the Nunnehi led the spirits of the dead. The West was the place of death.

After the white people came, Cherokee life changed forever. And the West was where they would be forced to go.

Chapter

A Black Cloud

Cherokee society was like most cultures. It changed and grew over the centuries. Cherokee meetings with other tribes were sometimes peaceful. And sometimes they weren't.

The Cherokee learned from the other Indians. In return, they taught other tribes their own special skills.

The Cherokee lived through good and bad times. They went to war, sometimes winning and sometimes losing. They suffered when there wasn't enough food. They grew healthy and strong during years of good harvest and game.

In bad years, illnesses would occasionally sweep through their land, killing many people at once. But in years of good health, population increased.

The Cherokee took these ups and downs as they came. As times changed, so did the Cherokee. They grew wiser and stronger with each change.

"This Immense Country"

But all of these experiences did not prepare the Cherokee for their greatest shock. That's when the first Europeans came to their land in the 1500s.

First came the Spanish. Then came the French. Finally, the English explored the area. Most of the Europeans moved on. But a few settled down.

Early Spanish explorers were looking for gold. When Hernando De Soto did not find gold, he was angry. He had some Indians tortured and killed. He hoped others would tell him where to find treasure. But there was no gold to find where he was looking.

Hernando De Soto

The French came looking for treasure too. But they also wanted land for their king. They were delighted with what they saw in the American Southeast.

The French explorer Pierre de Charlevoix said in 1721

> ⌁ The country is delightful. . . . As to the forests, which almost entirely cover this immense country, there is, perhaps, nothing in nature comparable to them. [They are greater than] everything of the kind we have in France. ⌁

Some Europeans admired the country. But some thought the Indians were godless **savages**. So since the Indians were not human, it was not a sin to treat them harshly. Some killed the Indians for little or no reason. Many Indians were captured and sold as slaves.

But other Europeans admired the Cherokee and their way of life. One Spanish explorer wrote that they were "a very gentle people."

A few Europeans settled with the Indians. They were the exception, however. Most explorers just passed through. They took what they wanted and left. Those who stayed usually lived apart from the Indians.

English settlers did not pass through as quickly as the others. They tried to stay friendly with the Cherokee. But they used the Cherokee just as the others had.

The settlers talked the Cherokee into fighting with them against others tribes and settlers. The English were interested in trading. And in some ways, the English traders caused more harm to the Cherokee way of life than the more violent treasure-seekers who didn't stay long.

The Cherokee were eager to buy or trade for the goods the English had. Because of this, the Cherokee way of life lost its **traditional** balance.

The English sold guns to the Indians. So hunting and killing became easier for the Cherokee.

Cherokee hunters became careless. They killed more game than they needed. They slaughtered deer and other animals so they could trade the hides for guns, alcohol, and other products. Some Cherokee even captured other Indians to sell to the English as slaves.

The Cherokee saw some things that they liked about white culture. With their usual acceptance of other people's customs, they took what they liked of the white people's ways. Some Cherokee became blacksmiths and traders. Others began farming the way the white people did.

Others changed parts of white culture to fit their own way of life. For example, the Cherokee had no written language. But a Cherokee named Sequoyah saw that reading and writing were useful skills. He invented an alphabet that fit the Cherokee language.

Sequoyah

At first, the white settlers and the Cherokee lived in peace. But few of the Cherokee stayed happy with the newcomers. What made them angriest was the way the settlers took any land they wanted. They made the Cherokee leave the places where their ancestors had lived for centuries.

25

Loss of a Way of Life

Traditional ways of life began to change. For instance, the Cherokee had believed that no one could own land. But the settlers staked claims and built fences. They made people stay off "their property." So the Cherokee started seeing land as something that could be owned.

Some settlers did not like the way all the Cherokee people shared power. In 1730, an impatient Englishman named Sir Alexander Cuming insisted that the Cherokee appoint a single leader. That way he would not have to wait for the tribal council to debate each matter. This changed the way the Cherokee had always made their laws.

Many Europeans did not think it was right for women to be involved in politics. The Cherokee leader Outacitty was taken to England in 1730. There he was introduced to England's leaders.

He looked around the crowded room. Then he asked, "Where are your women?" The Englishmen laughed at the idea that women could help make laws.

As a result, Cherokee women lost their importance as leaders. The Cherokee chief Wilma Mankiller (who may be a descendant of Outacitty) once said,

Outacitty

"One of the new values Europeans brought to the Cherokees was a lack of balance and harmony between men and women. It was what we today call *sexism*."

Not all the settlers wanted to destroy the Indian way of life. In fact, some thought that they were helping the Indians by bringing them "civilization." But in the eyes of some, these well-meaning people caused harm. **Missionaries** told the Indians that their religions were evil. The Cherokee lost many traditions forever when they became Christians.

The New World Meets the Old

The Cherokee chief Attacullaculla also visited England in 1730. There he met King George II. The king gave the Indians a **treaty** in which he promised to protect them "for as long as the mountains and rivers last and the sun shines." Most of the Cherokee trusted the great English leader to do what he promised.

King George II

But one of the great Cherokee leaders, Dragging Canoe, spoke for many of his people. He said, "Treaties may be all right for men who are too old to hunt or fight. As for me, I have my young warriors with me. We will have our lands!"

Other Indians sold most of Tennessee and Kentucky to the British. But Dragging Canoe warned the settlers, "You have bought a fair land, but there is a black cloud hanging over it. You will find its settlement dark and bloody."

Dragging Canoe moved into the hills with his warriors and fought the settlers for years.

When Europeans came to the Americas, they brought diseases with them. These diseases had never been on the continent before.

One of them was the deadly virus **smallpox**. In 1738, an epidemic of smallpox raged across the Americas. It swept through the Cherokee. Half of them died. Many of them died in agony. Some committed suicide. Many who survived the epidemic were left blind or terribly scarred.

The Cherokee were horrified at what was happening to their people. So they took England's side during the American Revolution. They hoped that England would win. Then the English would be grateful to the Cherokee for their help. Perhaps they would even live up to their agreement to protect the Cherokee.

The American Revolution began in 1775 and ended in 1783.

The angry Americans fought back against the Cherokee. Sometimes they **massacred** entire Cherokee towns. Whenever the Cherokee asked for peace, the settlers would not stop fighting unless they gave the Americans more land.

Then England lost the war. They were no longer able to help the Cherokee, even if they had wanted to.

Some Cherokee tried to make peace with the Americans. One leader was named Corn Tassel.

In 1777, American Major James Hubbard invited Corn Tassel and some other Cherokee to a peace council. The Cherokee were given an American flag to protect them from attack. They carried this symbol of freedom and justice. The Cherokee were full of hope and trust.

At the meeting, Corn Tassel and the other Cherokee took their seats. Suddenly, white soldiers leaped at them and hacked them to death with war axes.

There would be no peace talks.

Chapter

The Beginning of the End

Many Cherokee gave up on peace. They still loved their homeland in the Southeast. They disliked and feared the idea of the West. Their religion called it the place of death. But some Cherokee were so upset by their treatment that they moved west anyway. They settled in what is now Missouri in 1782.

President Thomas Jefferson said he thought the Indians would be happier in the West. There they would be away from the conflicts they faced with white people.

But some of the Cherokee refused to give up. They still tried to protect their land. They attacked white settlers.

In Tennessee, a young man named Andrew Jackson was nearly killed in one of these fights. For the rest of his life, Jackson thought Indians were untrustworthy savages.

Later, as president of the United States, he would become the Cherokee's most bitter enemy.

Meanwhile, President Jefferson told the state of Georgia they could make all Indians leave the state. This agreement was called the Compact of 1802.

The followers of Dragging Canoe could not make peace. In 1808, they took Jefferson's advice and moved. These people, who left the Southeast, became known as the "Old Settlers."

The Cherokee passed their own law. It stated that no Cherokee could sell land without all Cherokee agreeing to the sale. The Cherokee could kill anyone breaking the law. And the killer would not be arrested for murder.

Three years after the tribal law was passed, a Cherokee named Doublehead sold 8,000 square miles of Cherokee land in

The Ridge

Kentucky and Tennessee. He said the new owners had sworn that they would never ask for more territory.

An angry young man stood up in the Cherokee council. He said that Doublehead was wrong. White people would come back again and again for more land. Then no land would be left for the Indians. Doublehead was sternly warned not to sell any more land.

But he had not learned his lesson. Two years later, he sold more land to white people. The council remembered something. It was the far-seeing wisdom of the young man who had spoken at the earlier meeting.

The Cherokee gave the young man a new nickname. It was *Ka-nun-da-cla-geh*, or "Man Who Sees Farther than the Others, Since He Stands on a Ridge." He was called *The Ridge* from then on. In 1808, The Ridge killed Doublehead.

General Andrew Jackson grew impatient. The United States government wasn't making the Indians leave Georgia. The Compact of 1802 wasn't working.

Jackson told Georgia officials, "Build a fire under them. When it gets hot enough, they'll move."

But the Cherokee were still hoping to get Jackson on their side. In 1813, they joined him in a war against the Creek. The Ridge fought bravely. In fact, Jackson made him an army major.

A Cherokee chief named Junaluska saved Jackson's life at the Battle of Horseshoe Bend. He killed a Creek who had his war ax raised above Jackson's head.

Jackson and the Cherokee defeated the Creek in 1814. They took 23 million acres of land. The Cherokee asked for 4 million acres as a reward for their help. But Jackson refused. He also said that he thought it was time for the Cherokee to leave the Southeast.

The Cherokee felt betrayed. They had helped Jackson fight the Creek. One of them had even saved his life. If the general was still against them, who would help them?

John Ross

James Monroe

John Ross was the Cherokee leader. Ross was only one-eighth Cherokee. But he felt completely Indian.

When Jackson said that the Cherokee should move west, John Ross went to Washington, D.C. He convinced President James Monroe to sign a treaty allowing the Cherokee to keep some of their land.

Jackson heard of this agreement. And he was furious!

The Final Blow

Some Indians believed that if they lived more like the white people, they would have a better chance of being left alone. The Cherokee, along with the Choctaw, Creek, Chickasaw, and Seminole, were especially successful at living like white people.

Early 19th-century man's clothing,
Museum of the Cherokee Indian, Cherokee, North Carolina

Some white people called them the "Five Civilized Tribes." Many Indians found this term insulting. Angrily, they pointed out that all the Indians, not just five particular tribes, had an ancient and well-developed civilization. They did not have to copy the whites to become civilized. And in many ways, they were more civilized than their invaders.

But it was true that the Cherokee had picked up many things from white culture. Their form of government was now similar to that of the United States. They had a newspaper called the *Cherokee Phoenix*.

Many Cherokee prospered as farmers and traders. In ways, they were just like their white neighbors. Some even owned African American slaves.

Many Cherokee had become Christians, as well. Along with Christianity came schools. Missionaries were the teachers. Children from wealthy Cherokee families were often sent to **boarding schools**. There they lived and learned with white children.

But not all Indians wanted to live like whites. When the Bible was translated into Cherokee, a chief named Yonaguska asked someone to read part of it to him. Afterward, he said, "Well, it seems to be a good book—strange that the white people are no better, after having had it so long."

One Cherokee was especially angry that the whites thought their ways were better than Indian ways. He asked, "You say . . . 'Why do not the Indians till the ground and live as we do?' May we not ask . . . 'Why do not the white people hunt and live as we do?' "

Even if they had wanted to live like white people, the state of Georgia would not have let them. The government of Georgia began taking Cherokee property and giving it to any white person who wanted it.

A Cherokee would leave home to work in the fields, visit friends, or shop in town. When he returned home, white strangers were living in the family home. There was no way to get it back.

So more Cherokee gave up and moved west. Most of them joined the Old Settlers in what is now Oklahoma.

The worst blow to the Cherokee came in 1828. A Cherokee boy found a small gold nugget in a stream in Georgia. More than 3,000 people looking for gold invaded the area.

In July 1829, Georgia passed laws saying that no Indian could own property. The state took all of their land, including the gold mines. Cherokee schools were closed. Any Indians who objected found their property burned or stolen. Anyone who complained was jailed or killed.

It seemed that nothing more terrible could happen. But before long, the Cherokee were to discover that the worst was yet to come.

Chapter

"Get the Indians out of Georgia!"

By the 1820s, Cherokee life had changed. The Indians had given up their traditional houses and villages. They lived in log cabins and brick mansions instead. They had given up the idea that all people, male and female, should decide matters together.

Many had lost their traditional religion. Some had forgotten about a balance in life. They had been sickened and killed by new illnesses. Indian warriors had died in wars fought between white people.

The Cherokee were being treated poorly by the very people whose way of life so many of them had adopted. And at the same time, most of them had forgotten how to live the traditional life.

The Cherokee had given up their own culture. Now they were about to be stripped of their new one too. They were going to be forced from their homes. And there was nothing they could do about it.

Cherokee woman in front of cabin, 1800s Cherokee Indian Village, Museum of the Cherokee Indian, Cherokee, North Carolina

Resistance Grows

Many white people were shocked at what the American government was doing to the Indians. Famous American politicians,

Henry Clay

such as Henry Clay, Davy Crockett, and Daniel Webster, tried to make the president change his mind. But President Andrew Jackson had already decided that the Cherokee had to go. So he refused to listen.

The Cherokee were divided on how they felt about moving. Many still resisted moving. Beloved Woman Nanye-Hi said

⬬ *Cherokee mothers do not wish to go to an unknown country. . . . We have raised all of you on the land which we now inhabit. . . . This act . . . would be like destroying your mothers. We beg of you not to part with any more of our land.* ⬬

Old Chief Womankiller begged the Cherokee not to abandon their ancestors' graves. He said, "When I sleep forever, I hope my bones will not be deserted by you."

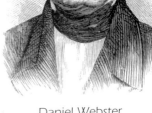

Daniel Webster

Many Cherokee had become so much like the white people that they didn't want to move to the Southwest for other reasons. They said, "fierce and powerful nations of Indians [lived] in the wildest state of savage **barbarity**" in the Southwest.

Other Cherokee thought the West was the only safe place for their people. By the 1830s, about 2,000 Cherokee had left their leafy forests and green hills for less fertile land in the West.

In 1829, President Jackson declared that all the Indians in the Southeast must be moved west. These included the Cherokee, Chickasaw, Choctaw, Seminole, and Creek Nations.

The United States Congress spent two long months arguing over whether they should accept this. Eventually Jackson's side won. In 1830, Congress passed the Indian Removal Bill. The bill forced the "Five Civilized Tribes" out of their homes.

The Supreme Court Ruling

It was not just Indians who were angry about the Indian Removal Bill. Newspaper articles said that it was cruel and illegal. Political cartoonists drew Andrew Jackson and his supporters as mean, greedy people.

Samuel Worcester

Two missionaries, Samuel Worcester and Elizur Butler, were angry too. They had spent years helping the Cherokee. Now Georgia was making them ask permission to visit Indian territory. They felt this wasn't right and said so. The two men were arrested.

The Cherokee Nation was a separate country. Therefore, people in the Nation didn't have to obey the laws of the United States. So the Indians helped Worcester and Butler.

The Supreme Court agreed with the Cherokee. The justices said the state of Georgia had no right to make non-Indians get permission to enter Cherokee territory. Chief Justice John Marshall ordered Georgia to release the missionaries.

Chief Justice John Marshall

Andrew Jackson

President Jackson was furious. So he did not force Georgia to obey the Supreme Court ruling. He said, "John Marshall has made his decision. Now let him enforce it." But Jackson knew that it was not the job of the Supreme Court to enforce laws.

Despite the Supreme Court ruling, the Cherokee had lost. Andrew Jackson was determined that they would leave their homes. He was even willing to break the laws of the country he governed to make sure that they left. He paid no attention to the people who objected to what he was doing.

A Last Desperate Attempt at Justice

The Cherokee leader, John Ross, went to Washington again. He tried to reason with the president. But he had no success. Chief Junaluska, who had saved Jackson's life at the Battle of Horseshoe Bend, went with Ross. But he, too, was ignored.

Jackson offered to pay the Cherokee for their lands. The amount was an insultingly low four and a half million dollars. Ross suggested twenty million dollars. Jackson refused.

But 300 Cherokee secretly signed an agreement called the "Treaty of New Echota." It said the Cherokee would move to the West for four and a half million dollars. This was the amount offered by Jackson and refused by Ross.

Many people, both Indian and non-Indian, were outraged. A **petition** was signed by 15,694 Cherokee. That was almost the entire adult population. It protested the sale, saying it was illegal. But the American government ignored them.

Rumors spread. It was said that the Cherokee were planning to attack any soldiers who tried to move them.

Brigadier General R. G. Dunlap of the United States Army was stationed in the Cherokee territory. At first, he believed the rumors. He prepared to do battle. But he realized that he was wrong. Dunlap said, "I soon discovered that the Indians had not the most distant thought of war with the United States, notwithstanding the common rights of humanity and justice had been denied them."

Martin Van Buren

Still, the soldiers used these rumors as an excuse to take away the Cherokee's weapons. Without their guns, the Cherokee were helpless.

Then all hope was lost. The president after Jackson was Martin Van Buren. He gave orders to General Scott. "Get the Indians out of Georgia, sir!"

Chapter 5

"All We Hold Dear"

General Winfield Scott was in charge of rounding up the Indians. He was an experienced soldier. He knew he had to act swiftly. And he did. The Cherokee didn't have time to plan.

Scott immediately sent a notice to the Cherokee. He threatened them with death if they did not obey his orders.

The Cherokee felt hopeless. They begged their friends, the government, and other Americans for help. But their pleas went unanswered.

More Cherokee gave up and moved west before they could be forced out. John Ridge was the leader of the Treaty Party, the largest group that decided to leave. He was the son of Major Ridge.

John Ridge

John Wool

John Ridge believed that the Indians would be forced to move anyway. Therefore, they should go on their own. They hoped the United States government would pay them for the lands and houses they left behind.

Ridge led a group of more than 400 Cherokee in March 1836. They joined other Cherokee already living in the Oklahoma Territory.

A United States general, John Wool, was in charge of helping the Indians leave voluntarily. And he was angry. His government wasn't paying the Cherokee for their homes or helping them with their move.

Wool wrote to President Van Buren.

> *If I could . . . I would remove every Indian tomorrow beyond the reach of white men, who, like vultures, are watching, ready to pounce upon their prey and strip them of everything they have or expect from the Government of the United States.*

One white person saw some Cherokee leaving by boat. He said

> *The parting scene was more moving than I was prepared for; when this hour of leave-taking arrived I saw many a manly cheek **suffused** with tears. Parents were turning with sick hearts from children who were about to seek other homes in a far off and stranger*

*land; and brothers and sisters with heaving bosoms
and brimful eyes were wringing each others' hands for
the last time.* ⌣

But John Ross still would not leave. By now, he had been chosen Principal Chief of the Cherokee Nation. He was respected by many people, both Indian and white. This great statesman trusted the United States government and the president to do the right thing. He was determined never to leave his home.

But the Georgia government took Ross's house and land away from him. Both were given to a white person. Ross had to pay rent to the new "owner" just to stay in his own home.

One day while he was out, his family was forced to leave. When Ross came home, he searched frantically for his wife and children. He finally found them on the side of the road. They had been caught in a rainstorm. Now he knew he had lost.

The Roundup

On May 10, 1838, the roundup began. On that day, General Scott led 10,000 soldiers from Georgia, Tennessee, Alabama, and North Carolina. They attacked the Cherokee in Georgia. People working in their fields, tending sick children, or going to school were rounded up. They were taken to a stockade. Anyone who tried to run away was clubbed or shot.

No one was safe from the soldiers. They burst into homes, schools, and businesses

and grabbed people. Frantic parents had no idea where their children were. Babies and sick people were left alone with no one to take care of them.

Even the dead were not safe. Bodies were dug up. Jewelry was stolen from them. Soldiers took whatever they wanted from homes. Then they burned the houses down. Children were captured. They were used to lure their parents from hiding. A few people managed to escape. But most of the runaways were killed or recaptured.

Some soldiers were ashamed of what they were doing. So they allowed people to escape. The soldiers in charge of the first 800 captured Cherokee let many get away. Fewer than 500 were left the second day.

Years later, Cherokee Rebecca Neugin remembered the roundup. She was only three years old on the day the soldiers came. But she never forgot it. She said

> *When the soldiers came to our house, my father wanted to fight. But my mother told him the soldiers would kill him if he did. So we surrendered without a fight. They drove us out of our house to join other prisoners in a stockade. . . . Eight of my brothers and sisters and two or three widow women and children rode with us. . . . My mother and father walked all the way.*

In one home, a woman patted the family dog good-bye. Then she gathered her children around her and got ready to leave. But before she could leave her cabin, she died. Some thought she died of a broken heart.

Chief Junaluska saw this sad scene. He wished he had let Andrew Jackson die in the Creek war instead of surviving to become the president of the United States.

With tears flowing down his aged cheeks, the chief said, "If I had known at the Battle of Horseshoe Bend what I know now, American history would have been differently written."

Farewell

The roundup ended on June 17, 1838. Of the 22,000 members of the Cherokee Nation, 8,000 had been captured. They were in stockades in North Carolina, Georgia, Alabama, and Tennessee. These prisons had been built quickly. So they were not very strong. And they were filthy.

There was not much food. Some of it was rotten. There were not enough blankets or places to sleep. No one had any privacy. Many people grew sick. Thousands died. Even before the move began, 2,500 Cherokee died in the roundup and in prison.

Then groups of Cherokee—sick, terrified, and angry—were led out of the stockade. They began the long journey to the strange place in the West.

A soldier named John G. Burnett wrote about John Ross's departure with his band. He said

> One can never forget the sadness and **solemnity** of that morning. Chief John Ross led a prayer. Then the bugle sounded and the wagons started rolling. Many children rose to their feet and waved their little hands good-by to their mountain homes. They seemed to know they were leaving forever. The trail of the exiles was a trail of death. Covetousness [greed] on the part of the white race was the cause of all that the Cherokee had to suffer.

Chapter

"The Cruelest Work"

In a letter written in 1840, John Ross's nephew, William Shorey Coodey, said that even the heavens seemed angry the day the Cherokee left for the West. At the moment they started moving—

> *A low sound of distant thunder fell on my ear. In almost an exact western direction, a dark spiral cloud was rising above the horizon and sent forth a murmur [like] a voice of divine indignation for the wrongs of my poor and unhappy countrymen, driven by brutal power from all they loved and cherished in the land of their fathers, to gratify the cravings of avarice [greed]. The sun was unclouded—no rain fell—the thunder rolled away and sounds hushed in the distance.*

Many Cherokee were Christian by this time. But they still thought that this unusual weather was a sign that the Cherokee gods were angry that they had to leave.

The Place Where They Cried

The Cherokee's trip to the West was badly organized. The earliest travelers went on filthy and crowded boats. Then the summer turned so dry that the rivers weren't deep enough for the boats to float. That meant that the Removal had to continue in wagons and trains and on foot.

There were many delays. Most of the Cherokee had to move in the winter. Food was scarce. And everyone had to deal with freezing temperatures.

In all the confusion, a fortunate few managed to escape. Some made their way back to the land of Tsali's youngest son in western North Carolina. This later became the center of the Eastern Cherokee territory.

But these Eastern Cherokee faced hardships themselves. They had to stay hidden. They didn't know what had become of their friends and families. And they were not sure which of their neighbors to trust. Years passed before some of them dared to come out of their hiding places.

The travelers faced a three- to four-month trip. Many were afraid of the West. It was the place of death. There were other concerns too.

The Nunnehi lived in the hills of the Southeast. How could they find the Cherokee in the West?

Ancestors were buried in the Southeast. What would their spirits do with no one to tend their graves?

The Cherokee were used to the green hills and fertile fields of the Southeast. How could they live in the hot and dry Southwest?

Perhaps worst of all, how could people they trusted, their friends and even their relatives, treat them like this? But this question and the others remained unanswered.

Reactions to the Removal

Very few Cherokee later wrote about their experiences in the roundup and the Removal. Most of them did not even like to talk about it after it was over. So historians have had to rely on records left by white people to learn about the terrible journey.

ECHOHAWK 1957

One white person who witnessed the Removal was Elizur Butler. He was one of the missionaries who had been imprisoned in Georgia. He traveled with the Cherokee to their new home in 1838.

Butler was a doctor as well as a minister. He did what he could to help the sick. Many people died of illness caused by the weather, bad food, and endless marching. Butler said the "Cherokee seem to be taken off as with a flood."

Old people and children suffered the most. Many children died, including Butler's own baby.

President Van Buren knew of these conditions. But he wanted Americans to believe that the Removal was successful. And he wanted people to think the Indians were being treated kindly. So he made speeches saying that the Indians were happy to move.

Many non-Indians knew this was a lie. In a letter to a newspaper in 1839, a traveler from Maine described the horrible conditions of a group of Cherokee who had stopped in Kentucky. People were dying on the frozen ground, the traveler reported. He wrote

We found the road literally filled with the procession for about three miles in length. . . . [They travel] on the sometimes frozen ground, and on the sometimes muddy streets, with no covering for their feet except what nature had given them. . . . When I read in the President's Message that he was happy to inform the Senate that the Cherokee were peaceably and without reluctance removed, . . . I wished that the President could have been there that very day in Kentucky with myself . . .

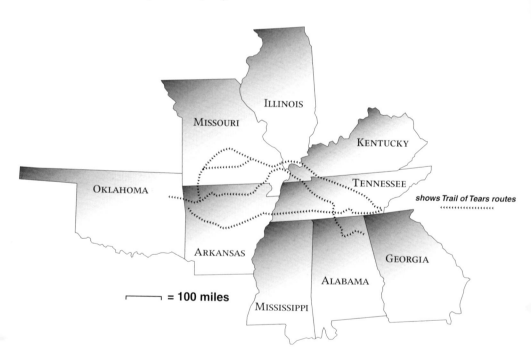

ILLINOIS

MISSOURI

KENTUCKY

OKLAHOMA

TENNESSEE

shows Trail of Tears routes

ARKANSAS

GEORGIA

ALABAMA

= 100 miles

MISSISSIPPI

Many white Americans felt ashamed of their government. They even tried to stop the march. But nothing they said made any difference.

Group after group of Cherokee continued to be rounded up. By now, the number forced out of their homes had grown to 16,000. The government kept saying that the Removal was necessary. And it was being done without harming anybody.

The Removal Continues

Each group of traveling Cherokee contained a few hundred people. They had to go about 900 miles. The trip took anywhere from a few weeks to four months. Supplies ran out. And it was hard to find farmers willing to sell them food.

People died of the poor food, the bad weather, and **exhaustion**. The dogs that came along with the Cherokee were starving too. As the walkers' feet bled, the dogs licked the bloody snow out of their footprints.

The wagons were pulled by hungry animals. They hardly had the strength to pull them. Wheels got stuck in the mud. So the people had to push them out.

As winter came, the mud froze around the wheels. This made travel impossible. Blizzards blinded people and caused them to wander off the road.

Small children tired quickly. Their parents were often too weak to carry them.

The Cherokee spent all of their money. Greedy farmers made them pay to cross their lands. Merchants charged too much for food, blankets, and medicine. They knew that the travelers had no other place to buy them.

Chief John Ross led one of the last groups to leave the Southeast. He had heard how difficult the trip was. So he tried to plan ahead to make things as easy as possible.

He divided his group into 13 sections. Each group had a leader and a doctor. Ross ordered blankets and food. But much of the food arrived spoiled. The blankets were not warm enough. The group set out hoping to make the journey quickly and safely. But they soon ran into the same problems that the earlier travelers had faced.

One night, John Ross's wife Quatie heard a child coughing. She went to help the little girl. She saw that the child had no blanket. Despite the freezing cold and blowing wind, Quatie gave the child the only blanket that she had. Quatie fell ill with **pneumonia**. In a few days, she died. She was buried in the cemetery of a family friend in Little Rock, Arkansas.

The last of the Cherokee arrived in the Oklahoma Territory on May 26, 1839. No one knows for sure how many Cherokee had died. But 16,000 had started the trip. And between 4,000 and 8,000 never finished it.

No one who took part in the roundup, whether Indian or white, ever forgot it. A soldier named Z. A. Zele said, "I fought through the Civil War and have seen men shot to pieces and slaughtered by the thousands, but the Cherokee Removal was the cruelest work I ever saw."

The misery, illness, and death that the Cherokee experienced on their long journey led them to call the path of their forced Removal *Nuna da ut sun y*, "the place where they cried." Today, it is known in English as "Trail of Tears."

Chapter 7

"A Revitalized Tribe"

The Cherokee's suffering was not over when they got to the Oklahoma Territory. For years, different groups of Cherokee fought for control of their new homeland.

Many Cherokee today are still fighting for control. They are also asking the government to restore much of their original land. Or they want fair payment for those lands.

The first group, the Old Settlers, had arrived in the West before the Trail of Tears. Many of the Old Settlers didn't want to share their power with the newcomers. They welcomed Ross's party. But they wanted it understood that their way of life was settled. The survivors of the Trail would just have to obey the current laws.

But the newcomers resented the Old Settlers. Many thought that the group should have joined in the resistance. Then maybe the whole tribe could have stayed in the Southeast. Soon they realized that even here in "Indian Territory," they would not be allowed to govern themselves. They would have to obey the Old Settlers. And that made the newcomers angry.

The two groups quarreled. Soon the fighting turned violent. One night, John Ridge was dragged from his bed. His dead body was found the next morning with 20 knife wounds in it.

John Ridge's father, Major Ridge, was also assassinated that same day. Elias Boudinot, John Ridge's cousin and editor of the *Cherokee Phoenix*, was murdered by other Cherokee. People suspected that Ross's group had killed these people.

Boudinot's wife warned John Ross. She said that some of her husband's relatives might try to get revenge for her husband's death. She told Ross to hurry to the fort for safety. Ross asked for protection from General Arbuckle, who was in charge of the fort.

A messenger carried this request to Arbuckle. The messenger rode so hard that his mule fell dead under him. He continued on foot. Fortunately, he managed to gather 50 soldiers in time to stand guard over Ross.

John Ross begged his people to stop fighting. He reminded them that Cherokee never warred against each other. Then he quoted the Bible. He said

Let us never forget this self-evident truth, that a house divided against itself cannot stand. . . . We are all of the household of the Cherokee family and one blood . . . embracing each other as countrymen, friends, and relatives.

Finally in 1840, the different groups agreed to stop the violence. They wrote a new constitution. It said that all the Western Cherokee were one united people. And it would not matter how and when they had arrived in the Oklahoma Territory. Old Settlers and survivors of the Trail of Tears would be equal. The battles finally stopped in 1846.

But some Cherokee, including Sequoyah, were still unhappy. They left for Mexico. They hoped to find other Cherokee who had gone there to escape the roundup. They were never heard from again. No one has any idea what happened to them.

Settling In

The Cherokee started making a new life in the Oklahoma Territory. They set up schools. There was even one for women. The Cherokee Female Seminary began in 1850. To have a school for women was very unusual. This was a time and a part of the country where very few women received much education. Elizur Butler became the seminary's first religious instructor in 1851.

The Cherokee adopted much of the way of life of their new white neighbors. It was just as they had done in the Southeast. They worked as cattle ranchers and salt merchants.

Many of them, however, had been wealthy landowners in Georgia and Tennessee. They had had slaves or servants to do the heavy work in the homes and fields. Others were people from cities or towns who had no idea how to live in this rough territory.

They now had to rely on their oldest family members. These elders still remembered how to hunt and trap for survival.

The Oklahoma Territory was different from the Southeast. Many of the plants and animals that grew there were new to them. Still, the grandparents' skills helped the tribe survive in its new home.

To the Present

In 1907, Oklahoma became a state. The Cherokee Nation was declared part of Oklahoma. It was no longer a separate country. That meant the end of Cherokee independence. They had no separate constitution.

Cherokee Nighthawk Keetoowah Society, display of beaded work and stickball team with their equipment, near Gore, Oklahoma, 1917

The Nighthawk Keetoowahs were led by Chief Redbird Smith, who was born along the Trail of Tears. Chief Redbird was dedicated to uniting all Cherokee and keeping their culture alive. The Nighthawk Keetoowahs held on to their own government until 1910.

Cherokee Nighthawk Keetoowah Society meeting, 1917
Standing left to right: Steve Sand, Jim Alex, Charley Scott, Bluford Sixkiller, Redbird Smith, William Rogers, Jim Hogshooter, Sam Lacy, Steve Cary. Seated: Peter Nix, Osie Hogshooter, Tom Horn

Cherokee Nighthawk Keetoowah Society, blessing the fire to be lit

Cherokee Busk Dance by Nighthawk Keetoowah Society members,
Gore, Oklahoma, 1924

Wilma Mankiller, Oklahoma, 1992

The Cherokee now had to obey the laws of the United States. These laws were to be followed even if they were different from what the Cherokee thought was right.

Wilma Mankiller was the first woman to be elected principal chief. She held the post from 1985 to 1995. The Cherokee Nation became stronger under her leadership.

Mankiller is the great-great-great-granddaughter of people who survived the Trail of Tears. She was born in Oklahoma. But she grew up in San Francisco.

Many Cherokee didn't want a woman to hold the position of deputy chief of the tribe. But in 1983, Mankiller was elected to the post. She took over as principal chief in 1985. She was later elected to a second term with over 82 percent of the vote.

In 1998, President Bill Clinton awarded Wilma Mankiller the Medal of Freedom. It is the highest honor a civilian can receive from the United States government.

Mankiller encouraged the Western Cherokee and the Eastern Cherokee to get together. Their first reunion took place in 1984. Since then, the two groups have held regular meetings.

Principal Chief Chad "Corntassel" Smith presenting his first State of the Nation address at the 47th Cherokee National Holiday, Tahlequah, Oklahoma, 1999

Wilma Mankiller is proud of the toughness of the Cherokee. She says that they have survived hardships that would have defeated many other people.

⌒*We are a revitalized tribe. After every major upheaval, we have been able to gather together as a people and rebuild a community and a government. . . . We are able to do that because our culture, though certainly diminished, has sustained us since time immemorial.*⌒

Cherokee children singing during the
47th Cherokee National Holiday, Tahlequah, Oklahoma, 1999

Chapter 8

A Cherokee Nation Today

In 1990, the number of Cherokee reached 308,132. Their Removal from their homeland had destroyed much of their culture. Today, only about 10,000 speak Cherokee. Much of their culture, religion, customs, and folktales have disappeared forever.

Cherokee woman using mortar and pestle, Cherokee, North Carolina, 1940s
From left to right: Mary Wolfe, Francis Wolfe, William Wolfe, Lizzie Tooni

The Cherokee are trying to save what is left of their civilization. "Land of the Blue Mist" is the Cherokee name for their 57,000 acres in North Carolina. The tribe bought this land in 1866. Today, this reservation is officially known as the Qualla. It is home to 10,000 Eastern Cherokee.

Since 1950, a play called "Unto These Hills" has been performed every year at the Qualla's outdoor theater. It is about the killing of Tsali.

The Cherokee Heritage Museum and Gallery in the Qualla tells the story of the Cherokee—past and present. Cherokee in the Qualla work hard to keep their traditions alive.

Remembering the Trail of Tears

The Trail of Tears still lives in the Cherokee's memory. Allison Shaw of the Alliance for Native American Indian Rights says, "The Trail of Tears is a real sore point. You learn to hate Jackson at an early age."

But some old wounds are healing. In 1992, the Georgia state legislature passed a resolution pardoning the missionaries Elizur Butler and Samuel Worcester for fighting against the Trail of Tears. The pardon was sponsored and accepted by Georgia State Assembly Representative Bill Dover, a Cherokee chief.

Other people deal with the terrible memory of the Trail of Tears by trying to pretend it never happened. Many books about Andrew Jackson have just a few sentences about this important part of his political career.

The Hermitage was Jackson's beautiful home near Nashville, Tennessee.

Today, it is a museum devoted to the former president. But the Trail of Tears is barely mentioned. In fact, a film is shown in the Hermitage's visitors' center. There is no mention of the number of people forced out of their homes, the horrors of the roundup, and the thousands of deaths on the Trail of Tears.

Photo of Cherokee Trail of Tears site,
"Rock Roe Landing Place," Arkansas, pre1933

But if Americans ever start to forget this brutal part of their history, a small reminder will keep its memory alive. This reminder is the Cherokee rose. It is the official flower of the state of Georgia.

A legend says that mothers of dead and dying children wept along the Trail of Tears. They neglected their other children and their own health. The chiefs prayed for something to happen that would make them less sad.

Their prayers were answered in a miraculous way. From that time on, whenever one of the mothers wept, a white rose would spring from the ground where her tear had fallen.

The golden center of the rose stands for the gold that was one cause of the Removal. The seven leaves on the stem stand for the seven Cherokee clans. The lovely blossom reminds everyone who sees it that even in sorrow, death, and despair, something beautiful can survive.

Glossary

ancestor   family member who lived and died a very long time ago

ancient   very old; relating to a time early in history

anthropologist   person who studies humans and their origins

avenge   to get satisfaction by punishing someone who has done wrong

barbarity   extreme cruelty; inhumanity

boarding school   place of education where meals and lodging are provided

enslave   to make a slave

exhaustion   condition in which a person is extremely tired and worn out

execute   to put to death

Ice Age   usually refers to the period that began about one and a quarter million years ago. It ended about 10,000 years ago. During this time, ice sheets covered large regions of land.

irrigate   to supply dry areas with water

massacre   to kill helpless people

missionary	person who teaches religion in hopes of converting others
petition	formal, written request made to an official
pneumonia	disease of the lungs
savage	person belonging to a untamed culture
smallpox	disease that causes skin eruptions; can cause death
solemnity	gloominess
stockade	pen where prisoners are kept
suffuse	to spread over with liquid or light; cover
surrender	to admit defeat; to give up
traditional	usual; customary; long-standing
treaty	formal agreement
vengeance	punishment inflicted to get even

Bibliography

The Cherokee by Elaine Landau. Franklin Watts, 1992.

The Cherokee and Christianity, 1794–1870: Essays on Acculturation and Cultural Persistence by William G. McLoughlin. University of Georgia Press, 1994.

The Cherokee Indians by Nicole Claro. Chelsea House, 1992.

The Cherokee Removal: A Brief History with Documents edited by Theda Perdue and Michael D. Green. St. Martin's Press, 1995.

Mankiller: A Chief and Her People by Wilma Mankiller and Michael Wallis. St. Martin's Press, 1993.

Night of the Cruel Moon: Cherokee Removal and the Trail of Tears by Stanley Hoig. Facts on File, 1996.

Selu: Seeking the Corn-Mother's Wisdom by Marilou Awiakta. Fulcrum Publishing, 1993.

Stolen Continents: The Americas Through Indian Eyes Since 1492 by Ronald Wright. Houghton Mifflin, 1992.

The Trail of Tears by R. Conrad Stein. Children's Press, 1985.

The Trail of Tears: The Cherokee Journey from Home by Marlene Targ Brill. Millbrook Press, 1995

When Shall They Rest? The Cherokee's Long Struggle with America by Peter Collier. Dell, 1973.

Wilma Mankiller by Linda Lowery. Carolrhoda Books, 1996.

Women in American Indian Society by Rayna Green. Chelsea House, 1992.

Index

Look for these other Cover-to-Cover informational books.

The American Revolution: Moments in History
by Shirley Jordan

America's Early Settlers: Moments in History
by Shirley Jordan

The Civil War: Moments in History
by Shirley Jordan

Pioneer Days: Moments in History
by Shirley Jordan